PART II

Compiled by Joan Frey Boytim

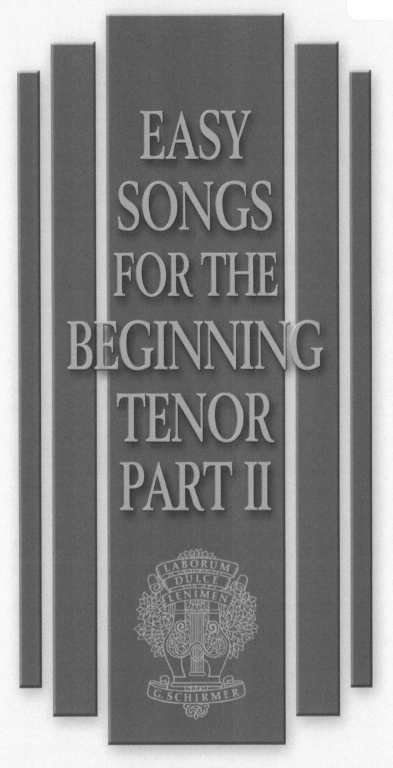

Laura Ward, pianist

ISBN 978-1-4234-1215-1

G. SCHIRMER, Inc.

DISTRIBUTED BY

HAL•LEONARD®
CORPORATION
7777 W. BLUEMOUND RD. P.O. BOX 13819 MILWAUKEE, WI 53213

Copyright © 2006 by G. Schirmer, Inc. (ASCAP), New York, NY
International Copyright Secured. All Rights Reserved
Warning: Unauthorized reproduction of this publication is
prohibited by Federal law and subject to criminal prosecution.

www.schirmer.com
www.halleonard.com

To access companion recorded piano accompaniments online, visit:
www.halleonard.com/mylibrary

4944-5495-0727-0854

PREFACE

The success of the books in the series *Easy Songs for Beginning Singers* indicates that there is a need for more preparatory literature of this type for middle school and high school singers in early stages of traditional vocal study. Teachers have commented to me that in some colleges these books are even used with very inexperienced freshmen, or with beginning adult singers.

The volumes of *Easy Songs for Beginning Singers—Part II* are at the same level as the original books. They can be used alone or in conjunction with the first set. Based on a teacher's choice of songs, there is no reason that a student could not easily start in *Part II*. Both volumes of *Easy Songs for Beginning Singers* lead very nicely into *The First Book of Solos* series (original set, *Part II*, or *Part III*).

There are 18-20 songs per volume in *Easy Songs—Part II*. A number of the selections have been out of print and will be unfamiliar to some teachers. All the songs chosen are very melodic and should pose no major musical or vocal problems for beginners of all types.

The compilation theory behind these volumes remains basically the same as in the original set. All songs are in English, some in translation, to keep the music easier to learn and comprehend. We have used songs with moderate ranges and tessituras to facilitate the building of technique. The wide variety of music includes folksongs, early show songs, operetta, parlor songs from c. 1900, as well as very easy art songs.

The art song composers include Schubert, Schumann, Franz, Arensky, Rimsky-Korsakov, Grieg, Quilter, Ireland, Head, Hopkinson, Beach and Dougherty. Operetta and vintage popular composers include Kalman, Romberg, Herbert, Berlin and Meyer. Care has been taken to provide the male voices with masculine texts. Some "old chestnuts" which young people may have never experienced include "Glow Worm," "Trees," "The Bells of St. Mary's," "Somewhere a Voice is Calling," and "Because."

My wish is that this set of books provides more options for the novice singer of any age, and helps all of my fellow teachers with the ongoing aim to lead more students into the joys of classical singing. Incidentally, these volumes may also be another source of relaxed and fun material for experienced singers.

Joan Frey Boytim
May, 2006

CONTENTS

4   BELIEVE ME, IF ALL THOSE ENDEARING YOUNG CHARMS

6   BENDEMEER'S STREAM

8   BILL GROGGIN'S GOAT

12   A BLACKBIRD SINGING

18   GREENSLEEVES

15   HARRIGAN

22   HOW CAN I KEEP FROM SINGING

26   I LOVE A PIANO

36   I WANT A GIRL

38   THE LARK IN THE MORN

40   MY LOVE'S AN ARBUTUS

44   O HEART OF MINE!

46   PASSING BY

31   A SAILOR LOVED A LASS

48   THINE ALONE

51   TWENTY, EIGHTEEN

56   THE WIND SPEAKS

58   YANKEE DOODLE BOY

BELIEVE ME, IF ALL THOSE
ENDEARING YOUNG CHARMS

text by the composer

Thomas Moore
(1779-1852)

way,_____ thou would'st still be a - dored as this
dear!_____ No, the heart that has tru - ly loved

mo - ment thou art let thy love - li - ness fade as it will;_____ and a -
nev - er for - gets but as tru - ly loves on to the close;_____ as a

round the dear ru - in, each wish of my heart, would en -
sun - flow - er turns on her god, when he sets, the same

twine it - self ver - dant - ly still._____ It is
look which she turn'd when he rose._____

1.

2.

BENDEMEER'S STREAM

Thomas Moore

Traditional Irish Folk Melody

Moderately slow

p

There's a bow - er of ros - es by Ben - de - meer's stream, And the
ros - es soon with - ered that hung o'er the wave, But some

night - in - gale sings round it all the day long; In the time of my
blos - soms were gath - ered while fresh - ly they shone, And the dew was dis -

child - hood 'twas like a sweet dream To sit in the ros - es and
tilled from their flow - ers that gave All the fra - grance of sum - mer, when

BILL GROGGIN'S GOAT

Southern Appalachian Folksong
Arranged by Richard Walters

A BLACKBIRD SINGING

Francis Ledwidge

Michael Head
(1900-1976)

ship ___ on the sea. ___ The _ song was for you _____ And the

ship, the _ ship was for me. _____

A black - bird sing - ing ___ I ___ hear in my trou - bled

mind, ___ Blue - bells swing - ing ___ I see in a dis - tant

wind. _____ But _ sor - row and si - lence _____ Are the wood's _ thren - o -

dy, _____ The _ si - lence for you _____ And the sor -

- row, the sor-row for me. _____ A

black - bird sing - ing. _____

HARRIGAN

text by the composer

George M. Cohan
(1878-1942)

Moderately

Who is the man who will spend or will e - ven lend? Har - ri - gan, that's
Who is the man nev - er stood for a 'gad - a - bout'? Har - ri - gan, that's

me! Who is your friend, when you find that you need a friend?
me! Who is the man that the town's sim - ply mad a - bout?

Har - ri - gan, that's me! For I'm just as proud of my
Har - ri - gan, that's me! Thy la - dies and ba - bies are

16

in me. "Di-vil" a man can say a word a-gin' me.

H - A - dou - ble R - I - G - A - N, you

see._____ Is a name that a shame nev-er has been con-nect-ed with,

Har - ri - gan, that's me!_____ me!

1.

2.

GREENSLEEVES

16th Century English Folksong
Arranged by Bryan Stanley

HOW CAN I KEEP FROM SINGING

Words possibly by Anna Warner

American Tune
Music possibly by Robert Lawry, 1869
Arranged by Christopher Ruck

3. When ty-rants trem - ble, sick with fear And hear their death knells ring-ing; When friends re-joice both far and near, How can I keep from sing-ing? In pris-on cell and dun-geon vile Our thoughts to them are wing-ing. When friends by shame are _

un - de -filed, How can I keep from sing - ing? No storm can shake my

in - most calm while to that rock I'm cling - ing.___ It

sounds an ech - o ___ in my soul. How

can I keep from sing - ing?

I LOVE A PIANO

text by the composer

Irving Berlin
(1888-1989)

Moderately

As a
When a

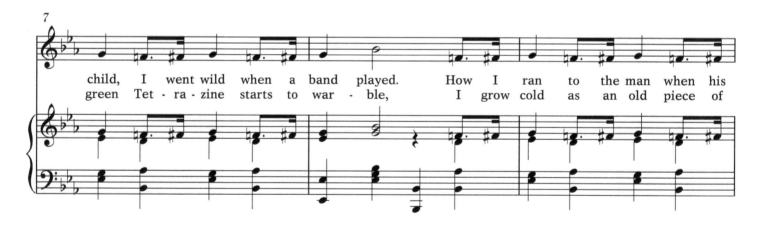

child, I went wild when a band played. How I ran to the man when his
green Tet-ra-zine starts to war-ble, I grow cold as an old piece of

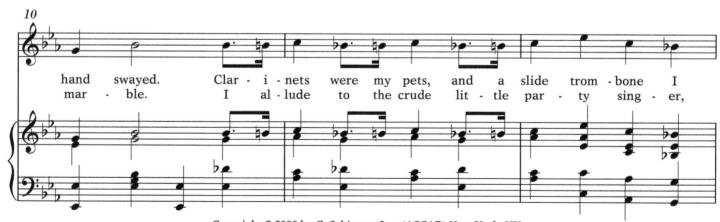

hand swayed. Clar-i-nets were my pets, and a slide trom-bone I
mar-ble. I al-lude to the crude lit-tle par-ty sing-er,

pian-o,_____ I love to hear some-bod-y play_____ up-on a

pian-o,_____ a grand pi-an-o._____ It simp-ly

car-ries me a-way. I know a

fine way to treat a Stein-way.

I love to run my fin - gers o'er the keys, _ the

i - vo - ries. _ And with the ped - al _ I love to

med - dle. _ Not on - ly mu - sic from Broad - way. _ I'm so de-
(Orig: When Pa - da - rew - ski comes this way.)

light - ed _ if I'm in - vit - ed _ to hear a

long haired gen - ius play._____ So you can keep your fid - dle

and your bow.__ Give me a p - i - a - n - o. Oh, oh, I love to

stop right___ be - side an up - right, or a high toned ba - by

1.

2.

grand.   grand.

A SAILOR LOVED A LASS

Stephen Storace

Old English Melody
Arranged by Henry Lane Wilson
(1871-1915)

49
yield - ed to de - spair,— But, noth - ing her grief as -

52
ff *p*
suag - ing,— She _ raved and tore her hair!_ At

55
f
length,_ worn out _ with sor - row, Un - a - ble to bear _ her

58
rall. *a tempo*
pp *ten.*
pain,_ She weds an - oth - er to - mor - row, As man - y will do _ a -
pp *colla voce*

I WANT A GIRL
(Just Like the Girl that Married Dear Old Dad)

William Dillon

Harry Von Tilzer
(1872-1946)

Dad - dy ev - er had. _____ A good old fash-ioned girl that heart so true, one who loves no-bod - y else but you. I want a girl _ just like the girl _ that mar - ried dear old Dad. _____

THE LARK IN THE MORN

English Folksong
Collected and arranged by Cecil J. Sharp
(1859-1924)

Allegretto con grazia

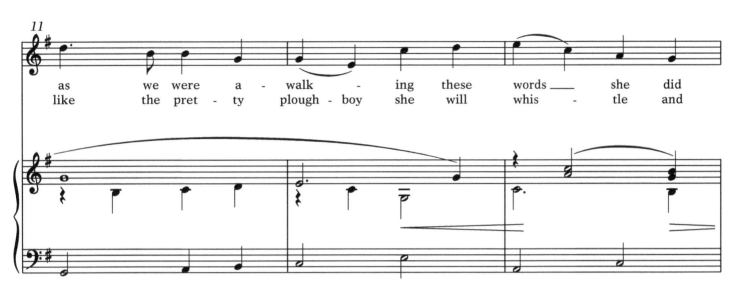

as   we   were   a - walk - ing   these   words ___ she   did
like   the   pret - ty   plough - boy   she   will   whis - tle   and

say: ___ There's   no   life ___ like   a   plough - boy's   all
sing, ___ And   at   night ___ she'll   re - turn ___ to   her

cresc.   *dim.*

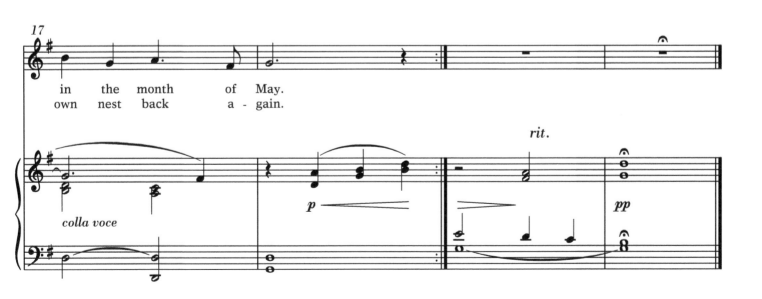

in   the   month   of   May.
own   nest   back   a - gain.

rit.

colla voce   *p*   *pp*

MY LOVE'S AN ARBUTUS

Old Irish Air
Arranged by
Charles Villiers Stanford
(1852-1924)

Alfred Perceval Graves

17
rall. [a tempo]

blue _ skies that spar - kle Through the soft _ branch - ing screen.

p

21
p legato

But the

legato

25

rud - dy the ber - ry And _ snow - y the flow'r, That _

29

bright - en to - geth - er The _ ar - bu - tus bow'r, Per -

33 cresc. f

fum - ing and __ bloom - ing Through __ sun - shine __ and __

cresc. f

36 dim. rall.

show'r, Give _ me _ her bright lips _ And _ her _ laughs _ pearl - y

dim. colla voce

40 [a tempo]

dow'r.

44 pp

A - las, __ fruit and blos - som Shall lie

pp

O HEART OF MINE!

Louise Heald

Henry Clough-Leighter
(1874-1956)

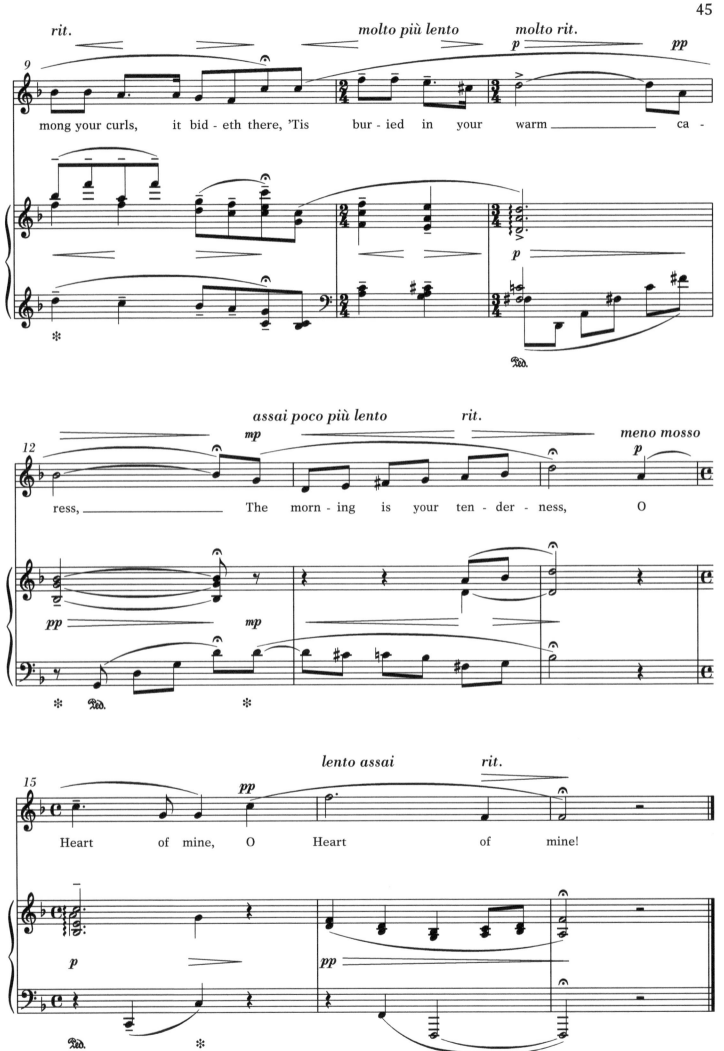

PASSING BY

Edward Purcell
(1689-1740)
Arranged by William Arms Fisher

THINE ALONE

Henry Blossom

Victor Herbert
(1859-1924)

won - drous to tell, 'Tis a rap - ture that's all di - vine! So with-

in thy ten-der arms en - fold me, For thy loss the world could not a -

tone! Be - lov'd I swear that I will e'er be true And for -

ev - er, thine a - lone! _____ Thine a - lone! _____

TWENTY, EIGHTEEN

English Folksong (Norfolk)

Transcribed and harmonized
by Deems Taylor
(1885-1966)

all shall be at your com - mand! ___ Twen - ty, ___ eight - een,

six - teen, ___ four - teen, Twelve, ten, eight, six, four, two, nought,

Nine - teen, ___ sev - en - teen, fif - teen, thir - teen, E - lev - en, nine and sev - en, Five,

three and one! Ho! What care I ___ for your rings and jew - els? ___ What care I for your

To Mrs. Florence Magnus

THE WIND SPEAKS

William H. Hayne

George Alfred Grant-Schaefer
(1872-1939)

Allegro con molto spirito

When I blow from the fro - zen north, ___ With an ic - y ton - ic

rife, ___ ___ My voice is a trum - pet, peal - ing forth, And I

shout of life. ___

When I

Andante con moto

YANKEE DOODLE BOY

text by the composer

George M. Cohan
(1878-1942)

Tempo di Marcia

mf

f

fz

p

I'm the kid that's all the can-dy, I'm a Yan-kee Doo-dle Dan-dy, I'm glad I
Fa-ther's name was Hez-i-ki-ah, Moth-er's name was Ann Ma-ri-a, Yanks through and

p

62